Norman Rockwell at Home in Vermont

Norman Rockwell at Home in Vermont

The Arlington Years, 1939-53

Stuart Murray

Images from the Past
Bennington, Vermont

Cover photo: Norman Rockwell's former home stands at the far end of the West Arlington Green, the second of two he owned in Arlington, Vermont, where he created some of his most famous paintings from 1939-53. *Photographer: Bob Burgess*

Back cover inset photo: With son, Jarvis (at rear) and a friend looking over his shoulder, Rockwell finishes the last "Willie Gillis" *Post* cover, showing the G.I. after the war, as a college student.

---

1 2 3 4 5 6 7 8 9 10 XXX 03 02 01 00 99 99 98 97

Library of Congress Cataloging-in-Publication Data
Murray, Stuart, 1948–
    Norman Rockwell at home in Vermont: the Arlington years, 1939-1953/by Stuart Murray.
        p.   cm.
    Includes bibliographical references and index.
    ISBN 1-884592-02-3 (pbk.)
    1. Rockwell, Norman, 1894–1978.   2. Painters – United States – Biography.   I. Title.
ND237.R68M86   1997   96-35007
759.13 – dc20   CIP

Copyright© 1997 Images from the Past, Inc.
Tordis Ilg Isselhardt, Publisher

Printed in the United States of America

Text: Adobe Garamond
Display: Castellar MT
Ornaments: Rococo Ornaments MT
Paper: 70 lb. Fortune Matte
Cover: 12pt C1S
Design and Composition: Macintosh 8100/80, with 172mb RAM, Quark XPress 3.32, Adobe Photoshop 3.0, Adobe Illustrator 5.5

Production: Open Press Interface between Stillwater Studio, Stillwater NY, and Thomson-Shore, Inc., Dexter MI
Scanner: Magitex 1875
Imagesetter: Purup Magnum
Press: (text) 40" Heidelberg Speedmaster ZP, (cover) 40" Heidelberg 501H-4C SM74
Printer: Thomson-Shore, Inc., Dexter MI
Cover Films: M&J Prepress, Albany NY

DEDICATION

For the people of Arlington, Vermont,
who remember Norman Rockwell

Moving to Arlington had given my work a terrific boost. . . .
Now my pictures grew out of the world around me,
the everyday life of my neighbors.

Norman Rockwell
My Adventures as an Illustrator

CONTENTS

Preface

Norman Rockwell was a native of Manhattan, a street-smart New Yorker by birth and upbringing, but he loved the country, where his family often went for summer vacations when he was a boy.

Country living always appealed to Rockwell, though he was not an artist who painted pastoral scenes, glorious sunsets or vast ocean panoramas. He painted people in action, always telling human stories in perfectly conceived moments of eloquent anecdote, moments crackling with vitality, moments he imagined and brought to life in his studio.

Though he was raised in a crowded city neighborhood, the charm of rural life stayed with Rockwell throughout his teenage years, when he was an artistic prodigy respected by his peers as the best among the best of his day, and even after he became successful enough to live and work anywhere he desired. At first Rockwell chose to stay in New Rochelle, N.Y., the suburban home of a chic, fast-living set of wealthy artists and writers.

By 1938, with a young family to raise, the excitement of that lifestyle had worn off, and Rockwell was looking north to Vermont as the longing for a quiet place in the country grew in him. That autumn he bought a farmhouse in West Arlington and the following summer he and his family settled down to live the next fifteen years with the folk of southern Vermont.

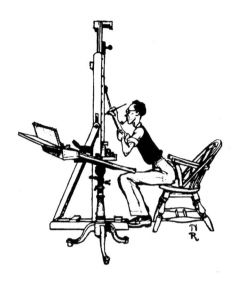

Immediately, Rockwell's style changed because his models changed. He became more than a slick illustrator with smart, sophisticated stories-in-a-picture. Now he was inspired to depict the everyday lives of his new friends and neighbors. His scenes were set in small-town diners and schools, in the back lots of half-forgotten old cities, and in homes, farmyards and doctors' offices that were familiar to everyone. The stories that Rockwell told so well in pictures went deeper now and became widely recognized images of the American myth. That myth was anchored by the belief that we are a decent people, blessed with honesty, inner strength and self-effacing good humor.

It was while Rockwell lived and worked in New England that he became America's best-loved artist, and it might be said that he was at his pinnacle during this time. Certainly, no other period in his long and productive career overshadows the legacy of those fifteen years, when Norman Rockwell was at home in Arlington, Vermont.

REGIONAL MAP

X ◂┽

A Visit
in Autumn

Late one afternoon in the fall of 1938, Norman and Mary Rockwell sat together on a bench in Arlington, Vermont, watching the people pass by on Main Street.

Norman puffed a briar pipe as his artist's eye saw the autumn colors of the wooded hillsides and how the Gothic spires of St. James Episcopal Church were etched against the twilight sky. This was the first time the Rockwells had visited Arlington, a rural community in the Green Mountains of southwestern Vermont. They had driven up from their home in the suburbs of New York City to look for an old farmhouse as a summer getaway.

COLONIAL INN. ARLINGTON, VERMONT

It had been a long day, spent with real estate salespeople in Bennington and Dorset, but the Rockwells had not found a place to buy. Disappointed, they intended to go home next morning after staying overnight at the Colonial Inn, an imposing 1848 Greek Revival mansion with a row of square columns across the front. Before having supper at the inn, the Rockwells decided to go for a stroll along Main Street.

Born and raised in New York City, Norman was in his mid-forties, prosperous and famous as one of the country's best illustrators. Mary was in her early thirties, a California native with Vermonters as ancestors. The Rockwells' three young sons had been left at home in New Rochelle while the parents went farm-hunting.

Arm-in-arm, Norman and Mary walked by the Italianate-style Canfield house, a handsome brick building far different from the simple white clapboard 1859 Town Hall next door. A little farther on, they passed St. Columban's Roman Catholic Church, built in 1876 and designed with a steep roof, board-and-batten siding and little ornamentation.

Nearby, Norman bought pipe tobacco at George Howard's General Store before they made their way leisurely back to the inn. He and Mary were tired, and the peacefulness of Arlington was welcome.

When "Happy" Bottom, owner of the inn, suggested they look at some farms the next day, the Rockwells decided to stay a little longer in Vermont. Norman had heard about the Arlington area from real estate man Burt Immen and from fishermen friends, who had praised the Battenkill River, a trout stream that wound down from the Green Mountains, flowing westward through the Taconic Range.

(Opposite, above) Named the Colonial Inn when Norman and Mary Rockwell first stayed here while house-hunting in 1938, this Greek Revival landmark in Arlington was built in 1849, and is today the Arlington Inn.

(Opposite, below) The east side of Main Street, with St. Columban's Roman Catholic Church, which would later become the Arlington Gallery featuring the Norman Rockwell Exhibition; farther down is Howard's store.

The west side of Main Street, Arlington, in the early 1950s.

A rugged region bordering New York State, this part of western Bennington County was patched with farm fields and pastures, hills heavily forested. The Arlington community, with about twelve hundred residents, was composed of three clusters of homes and businesses – the central Village of Arlington; the Village of East Arlington, a mile away over railroad tracks; and sparsely settled West Arlington, across the Battenkill.

The names of many Arlington families were prominent on local 19th-century maps. Some were among the first settlers, who arrived shortly after King George III granted Arlington's charter in 1761. Also living here were a number of professional artists and writers, musicians and poets, several of whom were very well known, though none as well known as Norman Rockwell.

The interior of George Howard's store on Main Street, soon after the Rockwells came to live nearby; pictured are Howard, behind the counter, Reverend George Brush of St. James Church, foreground; and clerks James Keough and Edward Burger.

By 1938, Rockwell's illustrations – on calendars, in books and magazines, tacked up on bedroom walls, often framed – were a familiar presence in the American home and had been for a long time.

During his twenty-six years as a professional illustrator, Rockwell had painted almost two hundred covers for the weekly *Saturday Evening Post*, the most popular publication in the country. Since his first paying work in 1912, his illustrations for stories and advertisements had appeared in every leading periodical: *Boys' Life, Literary Digest, Ladies' Home Journal* and *American* magazine.

THE WAGON WHEEL
MR. AND MRS. FRANK HALL
ARLINGTON, VERMONT
(Route 7)

ARLINGTON

R.R. STATION ARLINGTON VT

No one could tell a story with an illustration better than Norman Rockwell, best known for his pictures depicting humorous scenes from everyday American life. He had more commissions than he could easily handle and was always confronted with looming deadlines. For all his success, however, Rockwell was unhappy these days, worried about the originality of his work and about his ability to stay much longer at the top of his profession.

Troubled by more than just the uncertain course of his career, Rockwell was also weary of the fast pace of metropolitan New York, where he had spent most of his life. He needed a drastic change of scene, and both he and Mary wanted to spend summers in the country with their boys.

At the same time, Rockwell believed his work would be reinvigorated if he stayed a few months each year in rural surroundings without being distracted by the constant social demands of wealthy New Rochelle.

There was privacy and seclusion to be had in Arlington, yet a busy illustrator could get to clients in New York within a day.

Situated fourteen miles north of Bennington, a college town, Arlington was a station stop on the Rutland Railroad and was served by good highways. Eight miles to the north was Manchester, and an hour's drive to the west were Troy and Albany, N.Y. Brattleboro, a busy Connecticut River town, lay an hour eastward through the Green Mountains.

(Opposite, above) Originally a school, the Wagon Wheel Restaurant with its outdoor terrace was popular in Arlington; owner Frank Hall later opened the Green Mountain Diner south of the village.

(Opposite, below) During Rockwell's years in Arlington, the railroad station was a center of passenger and commercial activity, and clients would often arrive here on visits.

(Overleaf) A westward view of the Battenkill River valley, where artist Norman Rockwell and his family moved in 1939 from their suburban New York home.

Arlington was a thriving collection of small mills and factories surrounded by dairy farms. Fishermen, tourists and seasonal residents swelled the summer population and stimulated the cash economy, but Arlington was little changed by the coming and going of outsiders.

In the eighteenth century, when Vermont was a frontier claimed both by New York and New Hampshire, Arlington settlers had stubbornly clung to their land. During Revolutionary War times, Arlington was home to brothers Ethan and Ira Allen, leaders of the "Green Mountain Boys," militiamen who defended their homes and rights against all comers. The Green Mountain Boys were as quick to oppose a New York sheriff's deputies as invading British soldiers.

In those days, there was little regard in Arlington for the Continental Congress, which at first refused to recognize Vermont as a state. For eight years after the Revolutionary War ended, Vermonters conducted their affairs as an independent republic.

During the Revolution, Arlington farmer Thomas Chittenden was elected Vermont's first governor. Chittenden made Arlington his seat of government and the state's de facto first capital.

The day after strolling Arlington's Main Street, Norman and Mary Rockwell went with Burt Immen and his wife Dot to look at a sixty-acre West Arlington farm on River Road.

The Rockwells were immediately charmed by the beauty of the setting in the long valley of the Battenkill, leading westward to New York State. The plain farmhouse, painted white, had been built in the 1860s. It overlooked the Battenkill and had two red barns and an apple orchard.

An avid student of American history, Norman took interest in stories the Immens told him about this setting. As he stood in front of the house, gazing at the shimmering river, Norman saw an island where the only local killing had occurred during the Revolution. A lad had been stealing the cattle of the doctor who owned this land, intending to supply the Green Mountain Boys. The doctor had shot him, then discovered, to his horror, that the fellow was his former apprentice.

The next day, the Rockwells bought the farm, and went home to New Rochelle, delighted to have found a family "hideout" for the summers. They arranged for local builder Walt Squires to turn the smaller of the two barns into a studio. Even when Norman Rockwell was on vacation, he had to be at his easel, often eight hours a day, seven days a week.

The River Road house, with its outbuildings to the right, before the Rockwells remodeled the front one as a studio.

The Rockwell boys, (left to right) Tommy, Jarvis and Peter, on the
stoop of their first Vermont home, on River Road.

The Rockwell family first came to stay at the West Arlington farm in the summer of 1939. The boys – Jarvis ("Jerry"), eleven; Tommy, nine; and Peter, six – were seldom away from the Battenkill, where they loved to swim and fish.

As September approached, Norman and Mary were so content in Arlington that they decided to stay year-round. The Rockwells settled in permanently that fall, though the house had no central heating and they had never experienced a Vermont winter. They made plans for modernizing the house the following spring, and in the meantime heated the place with wood stoves.

Though he had been in New Rochelle for more than twenty years, Rockwell wrote, "I was never really happy there. But the hard-dirt farmers in Vermont – when I got with them it was like coming home."

America's
Illustrator

Norman Percevel Rockwell was born in New York City on February 3, 1894, growing up streetwise in the tough, raucous neighborhood around Amsterdam Avenue and 147th Street.

Norman was much like other boys in his crowd, running about in knickers, spitting down on passersby from rooftops, digging holes to China in vacant lots, climbing telephone poles and riding the trolley in a summer evening's excursion. He loved to draw pictures as his father read Dickens aloud to the family by gas lamp.

Norman came from a solidly middle-class Anglo-Saxon family. His father managed the office of a textile firm, and his mother was the daughter of an English immigrant housepainter who had aspired with some success to be a professional artist.

Perhaps it was the influence of this grandfather that made Norman stand out from his friends in one remarkable way: He often impressed his crowd by chalking humorous cartoons and pictures on the sidewalk, once drawing dozens of warships from Admiral Dewey's fleet, which had just sailed into New York harbor and was the big news of the day.

Norman loved his family's regular summer visits to the country, such a contrast to the grimy city streets. In some ways he idealized rural life, for he knew how cruel the city could be. More than once, Norman saw the underside of New York, as gangs brutally fought in alleys, and drunken men and women brawled with cops. In later years, he had no urge to depict what was bleakest in the human condition. His city childhood had revealed that only too well.

Many of Norman's friends had no way to escape their harsh lives, but he did. He was determined to succeed as a professional illustrator.

In his early teens, Norman showed enough talent in drawing to attend the Chase School of Applied and Fine Art two days a week. Later, when he was accepted at the prestigious National Academy, he dropped out of high school.

Eventually, he studied at the Art Students League, where he was admired as the very best among the country's best young artists. Famous alumni of the League were Winslow Homer, Charles Dana Gibson, and

Rockwell's hero, Howard Pyle, the greatest illustrator of "The Golden Age of Illustration" that flourished in the last half of the 19th century and the beginning of the 20th.

For all his rowdy early upbringing, which gave him a love for practical jokes, Rockwell was so serious in art school that his friends called him "The Deacon." He always worked hard, trying with every painting to create a masterpiece, and remaining just that dedicated all his life.

Rockwell swiftly rose to become one of the finest illustrators in a profession that was fiercely competitive. Magazine cover illustrators – "cover men" – were considered the best of all. Advertising illustration commanded the highest fees, and these clients were the most difficult to please, but young Rockwell took to it naturally. He depicted hundreds of selling scenes for manufacturers of socks, oil heaters, automobiles, desserts, and insurance companies. Among his major commercial clients were Jell-O, Edison Mazda, Massachusetts Mutual Life, Coca-Cola, and Hallmark.

Rockwell loved to work, spent grueling hours at the easel, and seldom turned down a commission. He never felt he could afford to stop accepting commissions and paint whatever he wanted to paint.

Soon after selling his first cover pictures to the *Post* in 1916, Rockwell married Irene O'Connor, a pretty schoolteacher, from upstate New York. They had met while living in the same boarding house in New Rochelle.

Thanks to the prestige of being a *Post* cover man, Norman soon became so successful that they eventually bought a fine home in New Rochelle. They made friends in a fast set, part of the Roaring Twenties crowd that included Zelda and F. Scott Fitzgerald. Norman and Irene

Rockwell got his start as an illustrator of children's stories, such as this one for "The Magic Football," published in *St. Nicholas* magazine in 1914.

led a debonair life, partying with people who enjoyed heavy drinking, yacht clubs and extra-marital whirls.

It soon became apparent, however, that their marriage was unhappy and loveless. It would also be childless. Irene liked to socialize, and was not interested in Norman's pictures. He, in turn, was too often working at the easel when his young wife needed his companionship.

By the late 1920s, Norman was depressed with the swinging life, but he kept up a prodigious output of work. Because his pictures were mostly of people in lighthearted situations, it was thought by those who did not know him that he was a fellow content with the world. He was not.

Rockwell was complex and driven, burdened with the anxiety that comes of ambitious genius. He strove for excellence and labored to exhaustion on nearly every painting. Though millions of Americans looked forward to his next illustrations, his mind was seldom at ease.

A worrier, full of self-doubt, Rockwell was afraid of drying up, of running out of new picture ideas. Throughout his career, he had painful phases of self-searching about his ability as an artist. As an obsessive perfectionist, he set extremely high standards for himself, admiring the old masters such as Rembrandt and Vermeer. His ideal, however, was Pyle, considered the master for Rockwell's generation of illustrators. He also respected some of the moderns, such as Picasso, for their originality and imagination.

Where, he wondered, did he fit in?

On a visit to Paris in the mid-1920s, Rockwell briefly enrolled at the famous Calorossi art school, trying to learn what was up to date. He wanted to understand "modern art" and the latest color theories, and for a while tried to adapt his style to make it more contemporary. It was discouraging because he just did not see things abstractly, the way "modern" artists did.

What he loved to illustrate were human subjects, realistically rendered, with a story clearly and skillfully told in each picture. He finally gave up at Calorossi when some admiring young art students came and asked his advice on becoming professional illustrators like him.

Despite his fame and financial success, Rockwell always had the need to find himself as an artist. He went to Europe several more times, visiting galleries and museums, seeking fresh perspectives. Irene never went with him, though. She preferred to stay home with friends and family.

When Rockwell returned from a trip to Europe in 1929, Irene met him with a demand for divorce, for she had fallen in love with someone else. They had been married thirteen years.

A year later, Rockwell was in California on *Post* assignments, when he met and soon married Mary Barstow, who lived in Alhambra, near Los Angeles. Mary was fourteen years younger than Norman and, like Irene, was a schoolteacher. Unlike Irene, however, she took great interest in his work.

By 1932, their first son, Jarvis, was born. Though Norman was happy with his family life, he struggled more than ever with his illustration style. Confused, searching for another point of view, he moved his young family to Paris that year so he could try again to see firsthand what "modern art" was all about.

During this time of experimentation and inner struggle in Paris, Rockwell completed very few paintings. It was unusual for him not to paint up to eight *Post* covers a year, but only one cover appeared during the eight months the Rockwell family lived in France. It shows a gendarme giving directions to a pretty woman.

At first, the Rockwells had planned to stay for several years in France so he could develop a "more modern" style, but Paris did not have what he was after. He was best – and happiest – with the the storytelling pictures he had always painted.

They returned to their house in New Rochelle with Mary expecting a second child, Thomas. Peter was born there in 1936.

By 1938, Norman was the unquestioned best (and best-paid) illustrator of his day, but now he worried about losing his place at the *Post*.

There had been recent staff changes and he did not get along with the new editors. He believed there was even a chance he would be dropped as the *Post's* leading cover man.

More than ever, Norman needed a drastic change of scene, and Mary wanted to get away from the New Rochelle social whirl. She was repelled by the society set, which seemed to want her husband's company only to round out the guest list with a celebrity artist.

It was a Rockwell model, avid Battenkill fisherman Fred Hildebrandt, who first suggested he visit southern Vermont, where life was more easygoing, the surroundings peaceful. The Rockwells began to look at Vermont real estate brochures with farms for sale, and that autumn, drove up to see for themselves.

3

"LIKE LIVING IN ANOTHER WORLD"

After enduring their first Vermont winter in 1939-40, the Rockwells felt they belonged in Arlington. It was said to take twenty years before outsiders were accepted there, but these newcomers were well-liked from the start.

The boys attended local schools, the first few years in a one-room schoolhouse in West Arlington. It was not easy to leave their friends in New Rochelle, but Jerry, Tommy and Peter soon became part of the Vermont community, as did their parents.

Mary and Norman built an entirely new life in Arlington, joining local organizations, attending town and school board meetings and going to

One of the few pictures ever taken of Rockwell's first Vermont
studio, shown with the barn adjacent; these buildings burned in
the spring of 1943, costing Rockwell his irreplaceable collection of
original paintings and props.

covered-dish suppers and dances at the West Arlington Grange. The family enjoyed long walks on the roads and trails around the property. They stopped at dairy barns to watch the milking, or leaned over fences to see farmers pitch hay into the horse-drawn wagons.

The Rockwells bought more land through Burt Immen, until their property included several hundred acres around the original farm, and on the east side of Arlington a stream-side cabin where Norman would go to

Finding the opportunity to relax that he seldom had in the New York area, Rockwell takes a stroll with his dog, Butch, past a West Arlington farm. *Photographer: Arthur Johnson*

work, in solitude, on studies. Sometimes tourists hunted him out at home, and the cabin was a convenient escape from nosy visitors.

Mary ran the household and worked closely with her husband. She was his first critic in the studio and managed his business and financial affairs. The Rockwells hired a married couple to help Mary with the cleaning, cooking and gardening, but she was always on the go. When a prop was needed or a young model had to be fetched from school, it was usually Mary who got things done on short notice.

In 1944, Rockwell bought this cabin on the Roaring Branch from real estate agent Burt Immen, and used it as a getaway when he wanted to avoid the many tourists who came to see the famous artist's home.

The Rockwells soon made many new friends, who ranged from farmers to doctors, shopkeepers to artists. Since the 1920s, an active community of musicians, artists and writers had been centered in the Manchester-Dorset area, a dozen miles north of Arlington.

The leading lights included poet Robert Frost and painters Reginald Marsh and Carl Ruggles (also a well-known composer). In the hills north of Arlington lived illustrator Rockwell Kent, who kept up a running correspondence with Norman over the years, each relating humorous instances of how one was mistaken for the other.

Mary Rockwell, in the 1940s.

Rockwell sketched these portraits of Arlington author Dorothy
Canfield Fisher and her husband, John, who were friends of Norman
and Mary, sometimes working together to organize arts events.

The most notable Arlingtonian of the day was author Dorothy Canfield Fisher, a founding editor of the Book-of-the-Month Club and a central figure in the region's cultural life. She became a friend of the Rockwells, and often gave them copies of the latest books under consideration by the book club.

More than once in those years, the opinions of Norman and Mary Rockwell influenced which new books were accepted by Dorothy Canfield Fisher's editorial board.

A major change came over Rockwell's career at this time, for he was unable to hire professional models and instead had to ask friends and neighbors, who were not used to posing.

This could have been a disaster for a lesser artist or one too temperamental to be patient with amateurs. It was testimony to Rockwell's skill and good humor that he could draw out what he needed from inexperienced models. At the same time, he discovered unexpected qualities that, to his delight, helped bring new freshness to his work.

Rockwell further developed a system he had recently started of having an assistant photograph models in black and white from every angle and in a variety of possible positions. Not even a professional model could hold some poses long enough to be painted from life.

Then the assistant would develop the film and print the photos, sometimes working late into the night so Rockwell could have them when he came to the studio at eight the next morning.

Photography was a blessing to Rockwell, but he did not just copy the photos. He worked from them for preliminary studies and sketches, interpreting them, and combining several photo images on one canvas. Dozens of photos were taken, and Rockwell's finished pictures were the result of skillful composition by the artist.

The artist shows young models the pose he wants for a Hallmark
card illustration depicting children running after the mailman.
Photographer: Gene Pelham

At work in the West Arlington Studio, Rockwell used many
photographs of models to work up sketches for the final painting.
Photographer: Arthur Johnson

A preliminary sketch of "Marble Champion," published in
September, 1939, the first *Post* cover Rockwell created after
moving to Vermont.

Rockwell's first *Post* cover painted in Arlington was of a girl playing marbles with two boys, and winning.

Soon, Vermonters who sat for Rockwell were thrilled to find themselves on the covers of magazines or in the advertisements and story illustrations. When modeling for Rockwell, the Vermonters came to appreciate his wit and kindness – though photo sessions could last for an hour and a half as he went after just the right poses.

The local models respected his hard work.

"Norman wasn't the type you thought of as a famous person," said Dot Immen. "He was one of us and so down-to-earth, such a modest man. . . . It was fun when you modeled for him because with his sense of humor he would laugh and have you laughing."

The Immens' six-year-old daughter, Mary, often modeled for Rockwell. On one occasion he needed her to be a hurricane victim rescued from a flood by a Boy Scout. Dot brought Mary to the studio in her best clothes, scrubbed and shiny, blond hair perfectly curled.

"Norman said I looked like I was going to a birthday party, not someone just saved from a flood," Mary Immen Hall recalled years later. "Off came the dress, shoes and socks, and Norman took me to the studio bathroom, where he soaked my hair with tap water then wrapped me in a quilt."

"There," Rockwell said, "now you look like a flood victim."

Many Arlington children appeared in Rockwell's pictures. Mary Hall said modeling for him became a "community-sanctioned enterprise, and was a legitimate excuse to get out of going to school for half a day."

Rockwell always painted as realistically as possible. When Marjorie and Larry Brush came with infant daughter, Ann, to pose for photos at his studio, they were dressed immaculately, as they would be when visiting the

doctor's office. Later, when they appeared depicted in a painting as patients at Dr. George Russell's Arlington office, Marjorie noticed Norman had painted the baby's bootie half falling off.

When she remarked on it, Rockwell said, "It was falling off when you brought her in, and that's the way I painted it."

People learned that whatever Norman was looking at might end up on the cover of the *Post*. Clarice Squires, one of his models, thought he saw things "the rest of us would never see. . . . All of a sudden, he'd see someone who was interesting to him, and it was as if he was composing a picture right there. I would always know what was happening by the look in Norman's eye."

Friends who were top-notch New York illustrators visited Rockwell and liked what they found in Arlington. Cover man Mead Schaeffer, who had known Rockwell in art school and New Rochelle, was an enthusiastic trout fisherman and loved the Battenkill.

As an artist, he was immediately taken by the new impulse in Rockwell's work. Rockwell said the privacy, the slower pace of life had something to do with it, but there was another important reason: The models were no longer professionals acting out a role. They were ordinary people, and Rockwell posed them as themselves.

Rockwell pioneered the arrival in Arlington of several other successful artists who followed him there. Schaeffer, the first, moved with his wife and two daughters to a farm a few miles from the Rockwells. Schaeffer was Rockwell's closest friend in this time.

(Opposite) This Rockwell studio photograph of the models for "A Scout is Helpful" portrays six-year-old Mary Immen being rescued from a flood by Boy Scout Horace Young; Rockwell created many illustrations for the Boy Scouts of America throughout his career.

Dr. George Russell's office in Arlington became the subject for "Visit to a Country Doctor," one of the "Norman Rockwell Visits . . ." series of *Post* illustrations; the patients are Arlington residents Marjorie and Larry Brush, with their infant daughter, Ann and son, John.

Post cover men Jack Atherton and George Hughes also moved to Arlington, and in time a circle of brilliant illustrators came to live and work there. They brainstormed about art and consulted on their work in progress, offering each other both inspiration and blunt professional opinions. Their families took part in the life of the community, often contributing pictures for exhibit in local art shows. Before long, these shows became known for their outstanding quality, and they were regularly announced in national magazines.

Don Trachte, young creator of the cartoon strip character "Henry," came to live in Arlington because he admired the top illustrators who were moving there. He considered himself fortunate to be "accepted as part of the gang."

"I just worshipped those guys," said Trachte, who with his family sometimes modeled for Rockwell.

Modeling for these illustrators became a steady source of employment from Bennington to Manchester, and the whole community took a new interest in the latest magazines.

Child model Yvonne Cross Dorr said, "We always waited for the next issue of the *Saturday Evening Post* to see who would be on the cover."

In Arlington, Norman Rockwell was settled down and happy as never before. He said Vermont "was like living in another world," and being there had given his work "a terrific boost."

That work mounted up, and the demands on his time increased so that Rockwell needed a regular assistant in the studio. He often had whole sets built for a picture, sparing no cost to come up with the right props – antique furniture, certain clothes or tools, even a live horse on one occasion. He had to have help to create the sets and take photos, but it took a while to find a regular assistant.

Tommy practices sketching in the living room of their West Arlington home while his father offers the sort of advice he also gave to the many young artists who came to visit him in Vermont.

One day, as Rockwell drove through West Arlington, wondering how to hire the right person, he saw a fellow with carpentry tools working on a cottage. When Rockwell approached the man to ask if he could do some work at the studio, they both were surprised to recognize each other.

The man was Gene Pelham, whom Rockwell had known in New Rochelle, and who had been a model as a child. They had not seen each other in years and Rockwell had not known Pelham was in Arlington. By

now also a rising professional artist, Pelham had recently bought the house and moved in with his wife.

As an artist, Pelham knew what was needed in a studio and could handle a camera well enough to photograph models while Rockwell posed them. Pelham needed work and was glad to accept Norman's offer, but more than that, Rockwell was his idol, "tops in the whole business."

Pelham would stay with Rockwell for the next fourteen years.

Rockwell assistant Gene Pelham, himself a *Post* illustrator, painted this portrait of his mentor and friend around 1950; the painting is from a photograph Pelham took in the second Arlington studio and shows the artist in his usual overalls and holding a painting stick and brushes.

THE FOUR FREEDOMS

In 1940 America, Vermont was nostalgically thought of as a secluded place to retreat from the crowded cities. Idealized images of life in rural Vermont were in sharp contrast to the looming threat of world war that overshadowed the country.

By the end of that year, fascist armies had captured most of Europe, and President Franklin Delano Roosevelt was warning Americans they might have to confront Germany and Italy with force of arms.

Early in 1941, Roosevelt spoke to the nation about four basic human freedoms that must be defended, freedoms that were the essence of American democracy: "Freedom of Speech," "Freedom of Worship," "Freedom from Want" and "Freedom from Fear."

These were the noblest of ideas, and Norman Rockwell had the compelling urge to portray them on canvas. No adequate concepts came to him, however, for the freedoms seemed too abstract to be put in a story-telling scene.

In mid-1941, everyone in Arlington felt that shadow of foreign war, and young men were beginning to join the service. (Eventually seventy-one would be in uniform.)

Still, life went on, and square dances were held at the West Arlington Grange every Saturday night from Memorial Day to Labor Day. The entire community joined in for these dances, so that automobile traffic jammed the narrow covered bridge over the Battenkill – fortunately the cars were either all streaming in or out at the same time.

Parked cars filled the broad green around the open-sided pavilion, where a five-piece "orchestra" was set up. Out on the grass, older folk sat in chairs to watch the dancers, and the elderly or ill stayed in cars that were brought close to the pavilion to offer a better view of the fun. Children ran and played on the grass.

Everyone pitched in, including the Rockwells, who helped organize the dances, sometimes selling the fifty-cent tickets or preparing hot dogs and soda pop served in the Grange. Norman often met his models and their families at the Grange Hall dances: Jim Edgerton, a dairy farmer who typified the strong young father; his son, Buddy, who posed as a Boy Scout; Dr. Russell, who was an ideal country doctor, and Arlington's sheriff, Harvey McKee, who portrayed a rural lawman. As many as two hundred local residents became models for Rockwell.

Seen through the covered bridge, the Rockwell house stands at the far
end of the West Arlington Green. *Photographer: Robert L. Weichert*

It was especially gratifying to Norman that his work was entering a
dynamic new phase. Wherever he went these days he noticed interesting
faces: at town meetings, in stores, the post office, passing on the street, and
at those dances.

Young Bob Buck, a sawmill hand from West Rupert, regularly came to
the Grange dances, and one evening Rockwell asked him to model for "Willie
Gillis," the typical army recruit. Willie was the average American boy who had
joined up to do his duty, and as a *Post* cover image, he instantly won the hearts

of Americans, who saw their own sons and brothers in this character.

On cover after cover, Buck was pictured as Willie: fetching a mail package of goodies from home, peeling potatoes, sitting in the servicemen's chapel, sleeping in his own bed while on leave, reading the hometown papers, and dreaming about girls.

Mead Schaeffer's pretty teenage daughters, Lee and Patty, were depicted as rivals for Willie's affection. He became so popular that reproductions of his *Post* covers were displayed wherever American troops were stationed.

By late 1941, as war raged over the rest of the world, Rockwell increasingly thought about F.D.R.'s "Four Freedoms." In fact, he found himself thinking about them constantly, and it frustrated him that he could not come up with a way to portray them.

Willie Gillis was fun to paint, but Rockwell wanted to do even better. More than any other wartime concept, he hungered to depict the "Four Freedoms" as images Americans could understand. He and Mead Schaeffer often talked futilely about how to picture the freedoms. Nothing seemed right.

If only he could discover the right image, Rockwell was sure it would be his masterpiece, but when it came to portraying the freedoms, even America's greatest storyteller with a picture remained stumped.

On December 7, the United States entered World War II.

Too old for military service, Rockwell intended to do his part for the war effort and joined the local civil defense volunteers. He knew, however, it was through his illustrations that he could do the most.

Rockwell had painted war-propaganda posters in World War I, and now he used his talents to create images that called on Americans to stand united once again. By mid-1942 he had painted a poster of a G.I. in a tattered uniform, firing a machine gun and running out of ammunition. "Let's Give him Enough and On Time," the poster slogan read.

Rockwell's Willie Gillis was a real inspiration for Americans, in part because he put a kindly face on the grim business of waging war. While Willie, the G.I., was on the lowest rung of the military ladder, model Bob Buck was becoming a naval aviator and was sent to the Pacific. Rockwell had to use photographs of Buck to keep on portraying him in new situations.

Although Rockwell went on with his regular load of commissions, he was becoming so obsessed with the "Four Freedoms" that he often could not sleep.

It was during one of those restless nights in mid-1942 that he finally got the right idea: At a recent Arlington town meeting, Jim Edgerton had stood to speak against plans for building a new high school to replace the one that had burned down in late 1940. No one had agreed with Jim, but they had let him speak. It was a perfect example of what "Freedom of Speech" meant to Americans.

Rockwell was thrilled. He realized he could picture "Freedom of Speech" as it was experienced and practiced by average Americans, using his Arlington neighbors as models. The same could be done for all the freedoms. He could portray these mighty concepts of human liberty in their most basic setting, the very setting Americans were fighting to defend.

Seen in his first Arlington studio, Rockwell's first World War II illustration was for this 1942 poster of a machine-gunner, down to his last bullets, with the message: "Let's Give him Enough and On Time."

Rockwell believed this was the best idea for a painting he had ever had. Indeed, he thought he could paint his masterpiece after all.

A few days later, he took preliminary charcoal sketches to Washington, D.C., offering the "Four Freedoms" ideas free of charge to the war department. He was flatly turned down. Though he went to office after office, showing his pictures to whoever would look, no one in government was interested.

The *Saturday Evening Post* was a different story.

Ben Hibbs, the *Post's* new editor, enthusiastically commissioned the paintings, and Rockwell promised to be finished in a few months. It would not be that easy.

Depicting the "Four Freedoms" on canvas turned out to be the most difficult challenge Rockwell had ever undertaken. It was one thing to have a basic idea, it was another to finish it just right. He began to run into frustrating problems of composition and story. As he struggled and the weeks passed, he began to doubt he had the ability even to finish one freedoms picture.

His hopes for a masterpiece were fast fading.

For all his past success, artistically and financially, painting did not come easily to Rockwell.

Like the great illustrators, whose works he collected – Howard Pyle, Frederick Remington, Edwin Austen Abbey, Gustave Doré, George Bridgman and Arthur Rackham – Rockwell was committed to accuracy. He took great pains to be authentic with regard to clothing, character and surroundings.

When, in 1935, Rockwell had been commissioned to illustrate Mark Twain's *Tom Sawyer* and *Huckleberry Finn,* he had gone to Hannibal, Missouri, Twain's childhood home. There, Rockwell had studied and sketched the houses, caves and river scenes where Twain had set his adventure stories. Rockwell even had bought clothes off the backs of local residents in order to dress models correctly.

That was the same authenticity he had to have with the freedoms – authenticity forged with a clear and direct message, readily understood at first glance. "Freedom From Fear" and "Freedom From Want" went the smoothest, but "Freedom of Speech" and "Freedom of Religion" did not take shape until many false starts had been thrown aside.

Rockwell worked even harder, but months and the deadline passed. The stress on him and his family was immense. Mary, in particular, bore a heavy weight.

Mary was her husband's sounding board, called over to the studio to look at the latest work in progress. She often sat for hours, reading aloud to him as he painted. Mary favored the classics and, in the course of the years, read aloud Tolstoy's *War and Peace* twice over. It was good for Norman that the solitude of the house on the Battenkill offered him isolation and quiet to work, but its remoteness sometimes meant loneliness for his wife, who had been raised in suburban Los Angeles.

In these years, Mary was always busy juggling Norman's business affairs while carrying out the endless chores of a mother of three. The native Vermonters were fond of her, and she was seen daily coming and going in the family's wood-sided Ford station wagon. She often read children's stories to the students in the one-room schoolhouse her boys attended.

For nine long months, Mary spent many hours without Norman as he struggled in the studio, close to nervous exhaustion, on the "Four Freedoms."

The concept for "Freedom of Speech" sprang from public
meetings held in Arlington, which typify the democratic tradition
all over America; Arlington's Carl Hess posed for this painting.

In January 1943, the four paintings finally were framed and put on display at the West Arlington Grange for the locals to see. Then they were crated and shipped to the *Post* headquarters in Philadelphia.

Rockwell's "Four Freedoms," published in four successive issues early in 1943, brought him international fame that no artist before or since has ever achieved. They were printed inside the *Post* along with essays by, among others, Booth Tarkington and Stephen Vincent Benét.

Later, the paintings were the centerpiece of a phenomenally successful government traveling show to sell war bonds, helping to raise $133 million. Reprinted by the millions as posters, brochure art and calendars (and in 1994 as postage stamps), the "Four Freedoms" are said to have been reproduced more than any other paintings in history.

Rockwell was brought to the pinnacle of fame, not only in the United States, but around the world, for the Allied nations also admired and understood his depiction of the "Freedoms."

In the spring of 1943, at the very moment his "Four Freedoms" were touring America, inspiring a nation in the distress of world war, Rockwell's studio burned down.

Everything was destroyed – original paintings by him and others, sketches, one-of-a-kind props, records, reference books – the irreplaceable treasury of his thirty-year career. Among the most cherished things burned in the studio fire were Rockwell's favorite pipes, but the very next morning, friends from Arlington showed up with replacements. It was a most welcome gesture of their affection for him.

(Page 50) Published in the *Saturday Evening Post,* this ironic look at the disastrous loss of his first Vermont studio is typical of Rockwell's strength of character; he "rose from the ashes," as he put it, and began over in a new home and studio a few miles away on the West Arlington Green.

My Studio burns

by Norman Rockwell

Tommy in pajamas gives the alarm. 1:15 a.m.

Wow !!!!

light and phone connections burned out

Off for the Fire Department

Here they come !!!

by the way, the kids were having the measles

Jerry, Tommy and Peter watch

Med Grover square dancer gets thrown

Fire Chief Safford sings "It aint gunna rain no more"

Everyone enjoys Spectacle 2 a.m.

Family bicycles rescued

Coffee and sandwiches till 5:30 a.m.

By the dawn's early light

us 7 a.m.

Norman Rockwell

A NEW
START

Rockwell was philosophical about the loss of his studio and everything in it. At first he had thought it was like "losing your left arm," but then he decided the fire was a blessing in disguise.

Without his props, costumes and reference books, he was forced to begin anew, to find a fresh, more contemporary perspective. His style was changing again, that change spurred on in part by losing his collection, and in part by his new enthusiasm for painting scenes from everyday life.

Less inclined to paint contrived studio images, in the mid-1940s he became more of a journalist. After the enormous triumph of the "Four Freedoms," he went around the country on *Post* assignments. His pictures showed young paratroop recruits traveling by train, scenes in President Roosevelt's White House waiting room, the swirl of a crowded Chicago train station at Christmastime, and a young soldier coming home to his family's Troy, N.Y., tenement.

There was more Willie Gillis, of course, and also "Rosie the Riveter," an homage to women working in defense factories. Other scenes from the home front included a mine worker proudly wearing two stars to show he had two sons in the service, and there were poignant images, such as wounded soldiers coming home and European civilians in the rubble of a city.

Soon after the studio fire, the Rockwells moved to another home, a large, 1792 colonial on the West Arlington Green, closer to neighbors for Mary's sake.

In a twin house fifty feet away lived Jim Edgerton and his family, who became close friends with the Rockwells. Daughter Ardis, a Rockwell model, was in Tommy's class at school, destined to be the salutatorian when he was valedictorian.

The Rockwell home was reached by crossing the Battenkill on the covered bridge, below which was an even better swimming hole for the boys. While a new studio was being built behind the house by Walt Squires, the old one-room schoolhouse (empty now that a new school had been built) on the green was temporarily converted to Norman's workplace.

After a stroll, Mary and Norman Rockwell pause at the door of their home on the West Arlington Green. *Photographer: Arthur Johnson*

When the studio was finished, it was large and attractive, with a cathedral ceiling, and lit by a two-story, north-facing window. Panelled in knotty pine, the studio was twenty-four feet square and had a darkroom, workshop and bathroom. Comfortable chairs stood before the fireplace, and a cushioned windowseat was built-in below the large window, which was screened by curtains across the lower section for privacy.

The studio walls were hung with paintings, prints, shelves with books, models of ships, sculptures and figurines. Suspended here and there were old swords and guns. A chest of drawers held newspaper and magazine clippings, letters and reference materials.

Rockwell's working area was always immaculate, even under the easel, which stood in the center of the main room. His equipment, paints, brushes and canvases all were kept in perfect order. Extra easels held color sketches or paintings in progress or prints of other artists especially of interest to him.

Rockwell worked undisturbed for long hours in the studio, but when he was ready, there was no shortage of family and friends invited in to voice their opinions of a picture. Especially in the final stages of a painting, he liked to ask people for their reactions.

Open-minded and keenly self-critical, Rockwell in this way tested the clarity of the story he was telling. He sought clarity from the first pencil

sketches of an idea to the modeling sessions with the photographer, and right through to the last highlight on the picture.

Because of Rockwell's exhausting efforts for just the right poses, photo sessions were demanding all around. Yet, the models who came to the studio felt like honored guests, whether they were adults or children. Rockwell had worked in Hollywood, making pictures of the day's most famous actors for the *Post,* but he always remained modest, treating his inexperienced Arlington models with kindness and respect.

In his studio behind the house on the green, Rockwell poses with "The Agricultural Agent," painted in 1948 as part of the "Norman Rockwell Visits . . ." series.

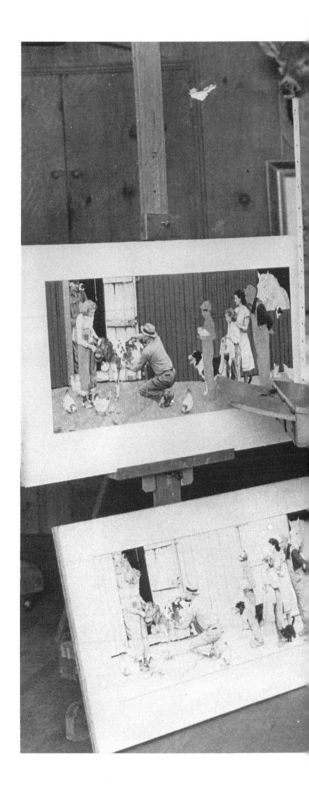

The artist poses a child in the West Arlington studio; on the easel
is the recently completed "Girl with Black Eye," and resting beside
it is a sketch for an unfinished picture depicting the peoples of the
United Nations – later to become "The Golden Rule," finished
in 1961. *Photographer: Bill Tague*

Rose Hoyt, a young mother, posed for both "Freedom of Speech" and "Freedom of Worship." Before starting on "Worship," Rockwell asked whether she minded being portrayed with rosary beads, as a Catholic, which she was not. She considered it thoughtful of him to ask.

Mary Immen Hall said, "I remember him making me feel important when I posed for him at six years old; it was the same for all his models.

"Norman Rockwell wanted his pictures to be right, but he cared about us as people, and I believe it shows in his work."

With photographer Gene Pelham following his directions, Rockwell in khaki pants and a flannel shirt would move around the models, deftly showing them expressions and poses. Alternating jokes with instructions, always with a precise focus, he explained what he was after and told the models the picture's story.

Rockwell at times was a model, himself, and was good at it. He was an able actor, and once played a leading role with Elizabeth Schaeffer in a community theater group.

It was during these years in Arlington that Rockwell first realized his original paintings were of interest to buyers.

In the past, he sometimes had painted over canvases after the images had been taken for publication. Once published, the originals had served their purpose and often were considered just so much clutter. Such large paintings as Rockwell usually created (some of them four feet by three feet, and meant to be reduced for the printing process) were too large for hanging above the average living room mantelpiece, so he thought they were no use to anyone.

In the loft of his West Arlington studio, Rockwell looks
over sketches that have been stored with finished
paintings and racks for canvas stretchers.

Often, he gave original paintings to other artists who could not afford to buy their own canvases and who were invited to paint over his. They did not always take his suggestion, and instead kept the painting untouched.

That his originals were valuable was proven to Rockwell when he contributed one to an art show in town. He liked the painting – the first of several April Fool covers, published by the *Post* in 1943 – and wanted to keep it, but out of politeness to organizers of the show, he agreed to exhibit it and asked Gene Pelham to bring it to town.

Rockwell insisted Pelham put a high price on it ($500) to make sure nobody would buy. Pelham took no chances and put a tag of $1,000 on the painting. To Rockwell's dismay, it sold to a wealthy heiress who happened to be browsing at the show.

Rockwell knew then that the many hundred paintings he had given away or discarded were worth plenty. Still, he continued to be generous with his originals, often giving them to models or to friends who liked them. He had no urgent need for cash, and it gave him pleasure to let appreciative friends have a painting.

He no longer casually overpainted a pictures these days, however, not unless he was unhappy with it.

World War II finally was over in 1945, and the young men came home to Arlington, which tried to get back to normal.

In commemoration of war's end, Rockwell created a powerful picture composed of many wartime images, showing humanity recovering, rebuilding, and impelled with new strength by their hope for a better world.

In October, 1945, just after the end of World War II, this *Post* cover, "Homecoming Marine," is set in Arlington's Benedict's Garage, where marine Duane Peters tells of his war experiences as Rockwell sons Peter, left, and Jarvis listen with local men – pipe-smoking John Benedict and brother Bob; Herb Squires, foreground, and Nip Noyes, right.

These days, Rockwell was happy in his relationship with *Saturday Evening Post* editor, Ben Hibbs, and worked well with new *Post* art director Ken Stuart. No living artist had been or was as famous as Rockwell, and his name had become synonymous with images of American life as it was lived by decent, ordinary people.

Those people were, for the most part, modeled on the folk of southern Vermont.

While average faces were the staple of Rockwell's production, the celebrities of the day considered it an honor to pose for him. Generally on assignment for the *Post,* Rockwell painted a wide range of film stars, such as Boris Karloff, Loretta Young, Ethel Barrymore and Lassie. He also painted baseball players Joe Garagiola and Stan Musial, United Nations delegates in New York, and leading American presidential candidates.

Some celebrities who were friends of the Rockwells traveled to Arlington for a visit, including entertainment mogul Walt Disney, actor Bob Cummings and actress Linda Darnell.

Relaxation for the Rockwells often included cocktails and dinner with the Schaeffers. With the boys, Norman built a tennis court that saw lots of use.

There were hikes up to Rattlesnake Rock on Red Mountain, and the family frequented Cordelia and Pete Comar's Quality Restaurant, Manchester, where a good dinner cost eighty-five cents. Rockwell liked to meet friends at Arlington's Green Mountain Diner or the Wagon Wheel Restaurant, with its outdoor cafe. Both were owned by entrepreneur Frank Hall, whose idea for a creating a tourist-trapping waxworks exhibit of the famous *Post* "cover men" was turned down by the artists.

The Green Mountain Diner was a favorite of Rockwell's and other professional artists who lived in the Arlington area.

To illustrate the diner's brochure, Rockwell gave Hall a sketch of a Green Mountain Boy carrying a turkey. The brochure was entitled "Facts and Folks in and About Arlington." It said the diner had works on its walls by Rockwell, Pelham, Atherton and Schaeffer, and curtains and waitresses' "costumes" that had been designed by Elizabeth Schaeffer.

Each year, the Arlington artists helped raise money for charity by drawing cartoon portraits at the village's street fair, held one Thursday in August. While Main Street bustled with dancing, pony rides and penny-pitch, several of America's most famous illustrators sat in a room over the post office, sketching away, charging a dollar for their doodles. The income generally went to the Community House or the library.

THE PINE ROOM

The decorations in the Pine Room represent some of the activities for which Vermont is famous, and show the work of some of her well-known citizens.

The short history of Arlington on the inside pages was written by Dorothy Canfield Fisher.

The photographic mural over the fireplace shows maple sugaring on the farm of Col. Fairfax Ayres. The picture which was enlarged to make the mural was taken by Gene Pelham.

The original oil painting "Partridge and Woodcock" was done by John Atherton. It appeared on the cover of "Sports Afield".

The four charcoal drawings on the west wall are by Norman Rockwell, done for the Brown & Bigelow Four Seasons Calendar.

In the glass case is a collection of the instruments used in maple sugaring, arranged by Col. Ayres, and a model which he made of the sap-house on Fayrport Farm.

The original painting of maple sugaring in Vermont was made by Meade Schaeffer for the cover of the Saturday Evening Post.

Our trade mark, the Green Mountain Boy with the wild turkey, was designed by Norman Rockwell; the arrangement of lettering on the menu was designed by John Atherton.

The skiis over the door were lent by Andrea Mead, fifteen-year-old member of the Olympic Ski Team.

The fishing exhibit was arranged by Meade Schaeffer. The rod was lent by the Orvis Company in Manchester.

The hunting exhibit was arranged by Lee Wulf.

The curtains and the waitresses' costumes were designed by Mrs. Meade Schaeffer.

All characters on the "Four Freedoms", "Gossip" Post cover and the "Family Doctor" cover are local people.

Your host, Frank Hall, is the gink with the derby on the Gossip cover.

~ Pine Room ~
Green Mountain DINER

FOOD WITH VERMONT HONESTY AND FLAVOR

Facts and Folks

in and

About Arlington

Rockwell drew the "Green Mountain Boy" illustration for the Green Mountain Diner's menu, and Dorothy Canfield Fisher wrote text for it.

My best wishes
To
Shirley Becker
Sincerely
Norman Rockwell

As busy as he was, Rockwell still found time to teach and encourage promising young artists who came to live in Vermont and work in his studio. They, too, were models from time to time.

"Christmas Homecoming," painted for the *Post's* 1948 Christmas issue and one of Rockwell's most famous pictures, depicted Mary, Norman and the boys and many friends from Arlington. Mary Immen Hall modeled for the painting, though she had sprained her ankle in school that day and had wrapped it in a white bandage. True to form, Rockwell painted her with the bandage.

In this picture was the elderly artist "Grandma" Moses, a friend of the Rockwells and a resident of nearby Eagle Bridge, N.Y. Though she was eighty-five when Rockwell met her, Anna Moses was just at the start of her career as a famous artist.

She painted colorful country scenes, working on her bedroom side table with housepaint on masonite, and using old jar lids for mixing colors. Grandma always marveled at Norman's spacious studio with its equipment for photography and for stretching or framing canvases, its wide variety of expensive brushes and paints.

One year Dorothy Canfield Fisher arranged a birthday party for Grandma at the Green Mountain Diner, just outside town. The party was broadcast nationally on radio, and with Norman's help Grandma cut a cake that had been decorated by the local *Post* artists.

Norman admired the freshness and vitality of Grandma's work, saying, "Her pictures are never phony. . . . They are good, honest pictures."

To him, that was the highest of compliments.

Arlington volunteer fireman Clarence Decker was a frequent model for Rockwell, who sketched this caricature for Decker's wife, Shirley, during a village street fair.

(Above) "Christmas Homecoming," a 1948
Post cover, shows the Rockwell family and many
Arlington friends; Mary hugs Jarvis while
Tommy and Norman look on, with Peter in
glasses at far left, behind Grandma Moses;
fellow-artist Mead Schaeffer is behind Tommy,
and Mary Immen is at the far right.

(Opposite) Rockwell decorates the
birthday cake for his friend and
fellow artist, "Grandma" Anna Moses,
whose party at the Green Mountain Diner
was broadcast on the radio.

The forties became 1950, and "Shuffleton's Barber Shop" appeared, inspired by the barber in Arlington. "Saying Grace," the picture considered Rockwell's most popular of all, was created in 1951: An old woman and a boy pray in a shabby railroad restaurant, with observant customers staring, some surprised, all of them respectful.

At this time the *Post* commissioned Rockwell to create a series of large pictures entitled "Norman Rockwell Visits," and his journalist's sense captured revealing moments in everyday American lives: a country school, a small newspaper office, a doctor's office, a farm visited by the agricultural agent, and a maternity ward.

Reflecting upon the wide popularity of these pictures, Arlington model Yvonne Cross Dorr said, "It is sometimes hard for us to believe the great amount of interest the rest of the world has in Norman's pictures of our small-town life."

In this time, Rockwell traveled to Washington, D.C., to paint the portrait of World War II hero General Dwight D. Eisenhower for the *Post.* Then a presidential candidate and future winner of the 1952 election, Eisenhower became a good friend of Rockwell's and sat for him more than once.

By now, television was competing with magazines, and photography had assumed ever more importance to the printed page, crowding out illustration. Yet, the *Post* was healthy, and Rockwell had plenty of commissions. Still, though he was turning out painting after painting that could be considered masterpieces, he was always wary of losing his audience.

Rockwell sits with Butch before a full-size charcoal preliminary sketch of "Saying Grace," the 1951 *Post* cover that is considered to be one of the most popular Rockwell paintings of all.

Rockwell was in his mid-fifties and beginning to feel old, haunted as ever by worries about his future. After a career four decades long, he had seen great illustrators vanish almost overnight, dying forgotten and in poverty. He did not want that to happen to him.

What he feared most was that his final legacy would be no more than that of a commercial illustrator, not an artist of the first rank.

Over the years, the Rockwells had often visited Stockbridge, Mass., a bustling Berkshire County town an hour's drive south of Arlington. Stockbridge was more populated and had a broad, fast-growing cultural scene.

By 1953, with the Rockwell sons away at school and headed for careers in the arts, the house on the green was too empty, too quiet. Mary and Norman felt restless. They needed a change in their lives, so that November, after fourteen years on the Battenkill, they left Arlington and moved to Stockbridge. It was the change in surroundings they wanted, but they were sad to leave so many friends.

It was just as sad for Arlington.

Neighbor Ardis Edgerton said, "We all did miss the Rockwell family when they moved. We thought they would be in the house by the covered bridge forever."

Rockwell, beside "Girl with Black Eye," modeled by Arlington's Mary Whalen, published by the *Post* in May, 1953, the year the artist moved from Arlington. *Photographer: Bill Tague*

AFTER VERMONT

From his new home in Stockbridge, Norman Rockwell produced several masterpieces in the early fifties.

In mid-1959, Rockwell and son Tom completed work on an autobiography entitled *My Adventures as an Illustrator*. Mary never saw it published, for in August she died in her sleep of a heart attack at the age of fifty-one.

Grief-stricken, Rockwell worked intensely, as he always did in times of personal crisis, and painted a portrait of Mary which was published on the dedication page of the autobiography. Then he painted "Triple Self-portrait" as a cover for the autobiography's first installment in the *Post* on February 13, 1960.

Rockwell was at the easel as much as ever, but was lonely and depressed. For distraction, he joined a local poetry group and there met Molly Punderson, a woman his own age, with whom he eventually fell in love. They married in 1961, with the warmest wishes of his sons and their families. A Stockbridge native, Molly was another former schoolteacher, as Mary and Irene had been.

Now approaching his seventieth year, Rockwell kept on painting, although the *Post* stopped publishing as a weekly in the mid-sixties. He was as busy as ever, painting mainly for *Look* magazine, and his work showed that uncanny timeliness, as always. He was more in demand with publishers than ever, despite some critics declaring he was not an important artist.

In an interview at this time, Rockwell told *Esquire* magazine, "I paint storytelling pictures which are quite popular, but unfashionable."

In 1967, he illustrated man's first step on the moon, a lifetime away from the turn of the century, when the child Norman Percevel Rockwell had sketched Admiral Dewey's flotilla steaming into New York harbor.

In 1976, after considering several cover ideas for *American Artist* magazine to celebrate the United States bicentennial, Rockwell decided to paint himself tying a "Happy Birthday" ribbon to the Liberty Bell.

The cover was published in July. It was his last.

On November 8, 1978, Norman Rockwell died peacefully at home in Stockbridge at the age of 84.

For Further Exploration

Places

The Norman Rockwell Museum
at Stockbridge
Route 183
Stockbridge, MA 01262
413-298-4100

The Arlington Gallery and Norman
Rockwell Exhibition
Route 7A
Arlington, VT 05250
802-375-6423

The Berkshire Museum
39 South Street
Pittsfield, MA 01201
413-443-7171

Norman Rockwell Museum
Route 4 East
Rutland, VT 05701
802-773-6095

Books

Buechner, Thomas S. *Norman Rockwell, Artist and Illustrator.* New York: Abrams, 1970.

Finch, Christopher. *Norman Rockwell's America.* New York: Abrams, 1975.

———— *Norman Rockwell: Three Hundred and Thirty-two Magazine Covers.* New York: Abrams, 1990.

Guptill, Arthur L. *Norman Rockwell, Illustrator.* New York: Watson-Guptill, 1946.

Meyer, S.E. *Norman Rockwell's People.* New York: Abrams, 1991.

———— *Norman Rockwell's World War II.* USSA Foundation, San Antonio, 1991.

Moffat, Laurie N. *Norman Rockwell: A Definitive Catalogue.* Stockbridge: The Norman Rockwell Museum at Stockbridge, 1986.

Murray, Stuart and McCabe, James. *Norman Rockwell's Four Freedoms.* The Norman Rockwell Museum at Stockbridge and Berkshire House, Publishers, 1993.

Rockwell, Norman and Rockwell, Thomas. *My Adventures as an Illustrator,* New York: Abrams, 1980.

Rockwell, Norman. *How I Make a Picture.* New York: Watson-Guptill, 1979.

Rockwell, T. *The Norman Rockwell Album.* New York: Abrams, 1961.

Walton, Donald. *A Rockwell Portrait.* Mission, Kansas. Sheed, Andrews and McMeel, Inc., 1978.

ACKNOWLEDGMENTS

Thanks to the many people who contributed to this book. First to Thomas Rockwell, who read the manuscript and permitted us to use his father's pictures.

In Arlington, special thanks to Mary Immen Hall, who gave generously of her photographs and her memories regarding the Norman Rockwell she knew during her youth. Joy and Henry Hinrichsen of the Arlington Gallery, with its unique Norman Rockwell Exhibition, shared with us the rich collection on display as well as an unpublished caricature drawn by the artist. David Thomas and Nancy Frank opened the extensive photo and printed ephemera archive of Arlington's Canfield Memorial Library and the Russell Vermontiana Collection to find historic photographs of the community the Rockwells knew.

Also thanks to photographer Bob Burgess for the cover picture of West Arlington, and to Irene Tague and Jeri Witt, who provided other important pictures. Linda Szekely, assistant curator of the Norman Rockwell Museum at Stockbridge, and Maryann Joyner, the museum's curatorial assistant, helped select many of the images essential to telling the story of Rockwell's life in Arlington, Vermont.

Michael Collins of the Rockwell Society of America and Paula Maynard of the West Mountain Inn gave us worthy advice and encouragement. Sincere thanks also to George Engel of Book Creations, Inc., and finally to editor Sarah Novak and designer Susan Mathews, whose solid professionalism helped transform an idea into a book.

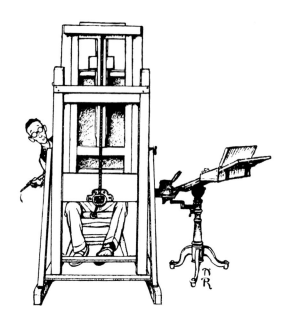

Sources of Illustrations

Front cover: Courtesy of the photographer: Bob Burgess, Arlington, Vermont

Back cover and pages 12, 22, 25, 37, 45, 58-59, 62, 71, 73: Courtesy of The Norman Rockwell Museum at Stockbridge

VII, IX, 17, 26, 28, 34-35, 48, 50, 64, 70, 80, 82: Courtesy of The Norman Rockwell Museum at Stockbridge. © 1996 The Norman Rockwell Family Trust. Reproduced by Permission

2 above, 6 below, 24, 32: Courtesy of Mary Immen Hall

2 below, 4, 5, 11, 67: Courtesy of The Russell Vermontiana Collection, Arlington, Vermont

6 above: Courtesy of Jeri Witt

8-9, 42, 66: Courtesy of Images from the Past Inc.

23, 29, 53, 54-55 and 57: Photographs by Arthur Johnson, Master of Photography and Craftsman, Courtesy of The Norman Rockwell Museum at Stockbridge. © 1996 The Arthur Johnson Estate, East Longmeadow, Massachusetts. Reproduced by Permission.

30: Courtesy of Pat Marohn. © 1996 The Norman Rockwell Family Trust. Reproduced by Permission

38: Courtesy of Gene Pelham

60, 75: Courtesy of Irene Tague © 1996 Irene Tague

68: Courtesy of The Arlington Gallery featuring The Norman Rockwell Exhibition

INDEX

(Page numbers with * refer to illustrations)

ABOUT THE AUTHOR

A book and magazine editor, and a journalist for twenty-five years, Stuart Murray has written nine novels and five works of nonfiction, including *Shaker Heritage Guidebook* for Golden Hill Press.

Murray co-authored with James McCabe *Norman Rockwell's "Four Freedoms,"* co-published in 1993 by The Norman Rockwell Museum at Stockbridge and Berkshire House, Publishers. His articles have appeared in *The New York Times, The Berkshire Eagle, The Albany Times Union,* and in trade and regional magazines. Scheduled for publication by Images from the Past in 1997 are *The Honor of Command: General John Burgoyne's Saratoga Campaign* and *Kipling in Vermont.*

Murray, who lives with his family in the Hudson Valley, has had a lifelong admiration for Norman Rockwell.

IMAGES FROM THE PAST

publishes history in ways that help people see it for themselves.

Another Images from the Past title you might enjoy:

REMEMBERING GRANDMA MOSES

By Beth Moses Hickok

Grandma Moses, remembered in affectionate detail as a crusty, feisty, upstate New York farmwife and grandmother by Beth Moses Hickok who married into the family and raised two of Grandma Moses' granddaughters. Set in 1934, four years before Anna Robertson Moses was discovered as an artist soon to gain national renown, the book includes excerpts from the author's diary and letters, treasured family snapshots, and an album of new photographs that evoke the landscape of Eagle Bridge familiar from Grandma Moses' paintings. The cover depicts a rare colorful yarn painting given to the author as a wedding present.

64pp, 9 b/w vintage photographs, 9 b/w modern photographs,
portraits of Grandma Moses in 1947 and 1949, and chronology
ISBN 1-884592-01-5 Paperback $12.95

Available at your local bookstore or from Images from the Past, Inc.,
Box 137 Bennington, Vermont 05201 (802) 442-3204.
For credit card orders, (800) 356-9315
When ordering, please add $3.50 shipping and handling for the first book and $1 for each additional. Vermont residents add 5% sales tax.